W9-ATO-033

Profiles in Greek and Roman Mythology

PERSEUS

Mitchell Lane
PUBLISHERS

P.O. Box 196
Hockessin, Delaware 19707
Visit us on the web: www.mitchelllane.com
Comments? email us: mitchelllane@mitchelllane.com

PROFILES IN GREEK AND ROMAN MYTHOLOGY

Titles in the Series

Profiles in Greek and Roman Mythology

PERSEUS

Susan Sales Harkins and
William H. Harkins

Mitchell Lane
PUBLISHERS

P.O. Box 196
Hockessin, Delaware 19707
Visit us on the web: www.mitchelllane.com
Comments? email us: mitchelllane@mitchelllane.com

Printing   1   2   3   4   5   6   7   8   9

Library of Congress Cataloging-in-Publication Data
Harkins, Susan Sales.
    Perseus / by Susan Sales Harkins and William H. Harkins.
        p. cm. — (Profiles in Greek and Roman mythology)
    Includes bibliographical references and index.
    ISBN 978-1-58415-558-4 (library bound)
    1. Perseus (Greek mythology)—Juvenile literature. I. Harkins, William H. II. Title.
BL820.P5H37 2007
398'.13—dc22
                                                                          2007000777

ABOUT THE AUTHORS: Susan and Bill Harkins live in Kentucky, where they enjoy writing together for children. Susan has written many books for adults and children. Bill is a history buff, who particularly enjoys the Greek classics. In addition to writing, he is a member of the Kentucky Air National Guard.

AUTHORS' NOTE: This is a retelling of Ovid's version of Perseus' life and adventures. Through the centuries, many details have been added, some by Hesiod. Although some details have become part of the legend, scholars don't know when they were added or by whom. Portions of this story have been retold using dialogue as an aid to readability. The dialogue is based on the authors' extensive research and approximates what might have occurred at the time.

PHOTO CREDITS: p. 6—Piazza della Signoria, Florence; p. 10—Tiziano Veccellio; p. 11—W. Russell Flint; pp. 20, 36—Sir Edward Burne-Jones/Staatsgallerie Stuttgart; p. 23—Castle, Prague; p. 26—John Singer Sargent/Museum of Fine Arts; pp. 28—Jonathan Scott; p. 30—Jean-Jacques-François Le Barbier; p. 31—Antoine Coysevox/Lyon, Paris; p. 33—Galleria degli Uffizi, Florence; p. 34—Pierre Mignard, Louvre; p. 41—Barbara Marvis.

PUBLISHER'S NOTE: This story is based on the authors' extensive research, which they believe to be accurate. Documentation of such research is contained on page 46.
    The internet sites referenced herein were active as of the publication date. Due to the fleeting nature of some web sites, we cannot guarantee they will all be active when you are reading this book.
    To reflect current usage, we have chosen to use the secular era designations BCE ("before the common era") and CE ("of the common era") instead of the traditional designations BC ("before Christ") and AD (*anno Domini*, "in the year of the Lord").

PLB

TABLE OF CONTENTS

Profiles in Greek and Roman Mythology

Perseus, the Gorgon slayer, stands triumphant. Using the tools of the gods Hermes and Athena, this humble youth cut off Medusa's head with a single but deadly blow.

PERSEUS

CHAPTER 1

A Supernatural Birth

In the torch-lit darkness, Acrisius (uh-KRIH-see-us) shifted his weight from one foot to the other. His journey had been long, and he was tired. Acrisius was a king, but standing before the oracle, he knew his place. He had bought his way to the front of the line, but he dared not rush the oracle.

He listened closely, but the words made no sense. The oracle might as well be talking the language of the gods, Acrisius thought.

At least it was cool in the small underground chamber. He had paid a good price to bypass the long line of worshipers snaking down the hill outside. Hundreds were baking in the hot sun. Farmers wanted to know if there would be enough rain for their crops. Barren wives wanted to know if the gods would bless them with a child at last.

Finally, the voice stopped. Acrisius waited in silence. Perhaps the sweet incense was helping him to relax, he thought.

Soon, a priestess slipped into the room. She understood the oracle's mysterious language. Showing no emotion, she spoke: "You have a daughter, and your descendants, through her, will rule a great nation. Be content. You will have no sons and your daughter's son will be your death."

The king gasped and stumbled back. "When? When will this happen?" he demanded, but the priestess had already disappeared behind the partition that separated him from the oracle. He dared not follow the priestess into the oracle's protected chamber.

From behind the partition, a voice replied, "When your time is done. Not before, not after."

He expected the oracle to tell him when this son and heir would be born. As a king, he needed a male heir, and he had only his beautiful daughter Danaë (DAY-nuh-ee).

In the cool dark chamber, his choice was clear. He must kill Danaë, and as soon as possible. He stormed up the stairs to the temple's main level.

Stepping outside, he raised his hand to shield his eyes from the bright sun. In the glaring heat, his situation seemed less certain. Perhaps killing Danaë wasn't the answer. She was nothing to him, that much was true. She had grown up in the women's quarters and he rarely saw her. It wouldn't bother him to kill her.

The gods were the problem. Gods powerful enough to send rain for the crops—or not, depending on their mood—were too powerful to ignore. He knew that the gods did not take kindly to mortals who harm their own kin. If he killed Danaë, the gods would punish him. They might even kill him. Most likely, they would send some horrible monster to devour him. The gods could be ruthless. Despite the searing heat, Acrisius shivered as he thought of the many ways the gods might strike at him.

As he traveled home from Delphi, his problem consumed him. If he could not kill Danaë, he must do the next best thing. He must make sure she never gave birth to a son—or to any child, for that matter. That might prove difficult for the king. Danaë's beauty was well known. Her royal birth made her a desirable match. Already, Acrisius was receiving proposals from kings and nobles across the south.

By the time he reached Argos, the king's plan was in perfect order. Immediately, he ordered his royal architects to design a large chamber fit for a princess in every way. He bought extra slaves so that it could be built quickly. He filled the chamber with the best furnishings. Colorful silks and linens draped the doorways and walls. Gold plates sat upon the tables.

In only one way was the chamber different from any other room in his palace. It was underground. There would be no doors or windows.

Only one small opening in the roof would let in air and light. To this plush but lonely dungeon, King Acrisius condemned his beautiful daughter. With Danaë inside, slaves secured the opening with criss-crossed bars of bronze. Guards surrounded the house night and day. Danaë could not get out. No one could get in. (During the European Renaissance, the story changes: The buried chamber becomes a tower.)

For days the people of Argos listened to Danaë beg for mercy. Days turned into weeks. Weeks turned into months. From Mount Olympus (oh-LIM-pus), even Zeus (ZOOS), the chief god of the Greeks, heard the girl's pitiful cries. Day after day, he watched the beautiful girl waste away in loneliness. Eventually the chamber fell silent.

Now, Zeus had a bit of a wandering eye. All the gods knew that he was unfaithful to his wife, Hera (HAYR-uh). Beautiful mortal women, especially ones in distress, were his weakness.

After watching Danaë pine for months, Zeus could resist no longer. He disguised himself as a shower of golden rain. By the light of a full moon, he poured himself through the bronze bars of Danaë's cage.

In the moonbeams, Danaë watched the golden rain fall through the opening. Gently, the soft golden shower encircled her. As it shimmered in the moonlight, she was mesmerized, even comforted. She danced in the warm golden drops. Surely this was a gift from the gods, she thought.

Fortunately for Danaë, the king had been a bit shortsighted. His plan would keep only mortal men away from his daughter. The lack of a door or a window without bars had not stopped Zeus.

Nine months later, Danaë gave birth to the son of Zeus. She named the boy Perseus (PER-see-us). For a few years, mother and child lived happily and undiscovered in the buried chamber.

Eventually, the sounds of the playing child reached the king. Danaë's secret was out. Despite the king's best efforts, his daughter had given birth to a son.

"Kill it! Kill them both!" he screamed in rage.

On Mount Olympus, Zeus heard Danaë's pitiful cries of despair. He turned himself into a golden shower and rained through the bars of her dungeon. Although Ovid tells of Danaë's loneliness in her chamber, in 1554, Titian painted the princess with a dog and servant.

Pleading for her son's life, Danaë told her father about the golden shower from the gods. She told him that Perseus was the son of Zeus.

"Liar!" he screamed at her.

Danaë sank to the floor and sobbed. Perseus patted his mother, as children do, hoping to comfort her.

Now the king was in a horrible rage. He was in mortal danger and the only way to save himself was to kill the boy. He felt no love for his grandson, but as the rage subsided, he came to his senses. Just as he couldn't kill Danaë, he couldn't kill Perseus, at least not without angering the gods. He contrived a plan—an evil plan.

"Carry a huge chest to the beach! Take my deceitful daughter and her brat too!" he commanded. "Put them both in the chest and cast them out to sea!" (Ovid's chest was bronze. Some later stories refer to a wooden chest.)

Acrisius Casts Danaë and Perseus into the Sea, painted by William Russell Flint, 1931. King Acrisius ignored Danaë's plea for mercy. He was arrogant enough to think he could change his fate by destroying his daughter and grandchild. Sources vary about Perseus' age when they were cast adrift. Some say he was just an infant. In other stories, he is a few years old.

Danaë struggled with the soldiers, but she was no match for the strong men. Effortlessly, they tossed her and her son into the chest. *Bang!* They slammed the lid shut and locked it. In the dark, Perseus began to whimper.

For a while, the two castaways clung to one another inside the chest. They were still on solid ground, or so it seemed. They were really on board a ship. Once the ship was so far out that the tide couldn't carry the chest back to the shores of Argos, they tossed the chest overboard.

King Acrisius watched from the ship as the chest became smaller and smaller, drifting out to sea. Once the chest sank, he would be safe. He didn't have to murder his own flesh and blood. The sea would take care of them.

How long would it take for the chest to sink? They will sink soon enough, he thought.

He had outwitted the gods and escaped his fate and there was nothing the gods could do about it—or so he thought.

In their tiny ark, Danaë and her child drifted through the night. Danaë listened to the waves wash over them. She sang to her son in the darkness to quiet him. At first, she was relieved when the chest didn't sink. Now she feared it was just a matter of time. Eventually, the ocean would suck them down to a cold, watery grave.

How would she console her son when the time came?

Why had her father abandoned her?

Why had Zeus abandoned his son?

As all mortals did, and like her father, Danaë would learn the truth of her situation, but only when the gods were ready.

The Fates

Atropos, Lachesis, and Clotho

The ancient Greeks believed that mortal lives were designed and planned by the gods. There was no escaping destiny, or fate. The Greeks believed there were three Fates, the daughters of Night. These sisters lived in a cave where they spun the thread of a person's life. The first sister, Clotho (KLOH-thoh), spun the thread when the person was born. Lachesis (LAH-keh-sis), the second sister, then drew the thread out. The drawn-out thread represented the person's life. After a time, the third sister, Atropos (AA-troh-pohs), cut the thread. This third sister was the most dreaded of the three. When she cut the thread, the person's life was over. She wasn't a goddess of death, but she did end each life at its appointed time.

Fate wasn't just for mortal men. Even the gods had to live by the rules. If someone was destined to die, the gods could not stop it. That doesn't mean they didn't try to interfere, because they did. It just means that in the end, they had to give in to Atropos.

In Perseus' case, Zeus or some other god may have had a hand in beaching the chest on friendly shores. It wasn't his fate to drown in that chest. That's not always the case. Sarpedon, the son of Zeus and Laodameia, fought during the Trojan War, as told in the *Iliad*, by Homer. When Sarpedon met Patroclus in battle, Zeus was tempted to spare his son's life. Hera reminded Zeus that other gods also had sons fighting in the war. If he spared Sarpedon, other gods would also spare their sons. Zeus saw her wisdom and let Sarpedon meet his fate, but he sent a shower of bloody raindrops to express his grief.[1]

The ancient Greeks didn't use the Fates as an excuse to do as they pleased. Rather, the Fates gave them courage, because they felt they weren't alone. They were freer to undertake tasks that they might not have on their own. "If the Fates will it . . . ," they were apt to say before embarking on some new adventure.

Zeus, the most important of the Greek gods, had an eye for mortal women in distress. He produced a number of half-god, half-mortal children, including Perseus.

PERSEUS

CHAPTER 2

Out of the Sea

For a second time where Danaë was concerned, King Acrisius had been shortsighted. First, he locked her away in a dungeon thinking only to keep mortal men away from her. Now he was content to let nature deal with his problem. In both cases, he never considered how the gods might be interacting with his drama.

The gods did not care when Acrisius locked up his daughter. In fact, Zeus, smitten by the young girl, enjoyed spying on her. This time the gods felt differently. From Mount Olympus, Zeus watched as the insignificant king tossed his son into the ocean to drown. Mount Olympus quaked with Zeus' rage.

One might expect Zeus to just reach down and pluck the chest out of the sea, but he could not do that. At this point, his wife, Hera, did not know about Perseus. Zeus hoped to keep it that way. Hera was the most jealous and spiteful of all the goddesses. It would not help Zeus or Perseus if Hera learned about the boy.

Still, the chest did not sink. Perhaps the hand of Zeus kept the small boat afloat.

Inside the chest, mother and child listened to the gentle swells smacking their tomb. They were lucky that the weather was mild—or maybe Zeus' brother Poseidon (poh-SY-dun), god of the seas, was also watching over them. The sounds of the soft waves were peaceful and comforting. Danaë and her child drifted until morning—although they had no way of knowing what time it was inside the dark chest.

Then Danaë noticed they were going faster. It seemed as if something was pushing or dragging the chest. The swells grew higher. She wondered if the weather was turning bad. After a while, she realized that the small chest was rocking forward on the tide, nearing shore. Danaë feared to hope too much. All she could do was wait.

With a soft thud, the sea finally dropped the chest on solid ground. What she could not know at the time was that the tide had beached the chest on the island of Seriphos (SAYR-ih-fohs) in the middle of the Aegean Sea.

Danaë now had a new problem. She was relieved that they were safely out of the water, but how could they escape the chest? It was locked from the outside.

The two did not wait long on the beach. Within minutes, Danaë caught her breath when someone rattled the lock. Suddenly, bright sunlight burst through the darkness and filled the chest. Arms reached inside and pulled the child and then Danaë from the box. They were rescued!

Danaë and Perseus stood on a beach, squinting in the warm sun. Standing with them was a fisherman named Dictys (DIK-tis), who had found the beached chest.

The fisherman took the mysterious pair home to his wife, Clymene (KLY-meh-nee). Having no children of their own, the couple took the castaways in and cared for them. Danaë and Perseus finally found the home they had never had with her father.

As the boy grew, Dictys took him fishing to teach him the trade. From the sea, Perseus learned courage and confidence. Often, the fishermen sang songs about a hideous creature named Medusa (muh-DOO-suh). She was the only mortal of the three Gorgons (GOR-gons). They lived in the Libyan Desert far to the south (known today as the Sahara Desert). Medusa was supposedly so ugly that no mortal could look at her and live. That added to her mystery and the terror they all felt at the possibility of actually confronting such a monster.

On fish, stories, and love, Perseus grew to manhood. One might think they all lived happily ever after, but they did not.

Danaë's beauty never waned. After many years, she was still the most beautiful woman on the island. Unfortunately, she was too beautiful to escape the attentions of the island's king, Polydectes (pah-lee-DEK-teez).

The king was Dictys' brother, but the two were nothing alike. Everything Danaë loved about Dictys—his kindness and loyalty—Polydectes lacked. The king was as cruel and selfish as Dictys was gentle and generous. In fact, he was very much like Acrisius, except he was even more arrogant. Danaë wanted nothing to do with Polydectes. She took great care to avoid him.

Even so, Polydectes became obsessed with Danaë. It is doubtful the king truly loved her. Most likely, he was in love with her beauty and wished to possess her.[1]

A dozen times or more, Polydectes commanded Danaë to marry him. She always refused. She was careful to pay him the proper respect. The last thing she wanted to do was anger another king!

Perseus stood fast with his mother against the king. Polydectes began to see that as long as Perseus was around, Danaë would never accept him as her husband. He must get rid of Perseus.

Arrogance will often blind one to truth. It is unlikely that Danaë would have ever warmed to Polydectes. She was quite content in her home with Dictys and Clymene. The only way Polydectes would ever make Danaë his wife was to use brute force.

When commanding Danaë did not work, the king turned to deceit. He began to spend time with Perseus. He would invite Perseus to the palace, and they often ate together. Perseus met important men while with the king.

One day, Polydectes announced that he intended to take a new wife (he had several already). He called all his friends, which now included Perseus, together for a celebration. At the gathering, each guest brought a gift for the bride-to-be, as was the custom.

Perseus had nothing to offer and Polydectes knew it. The king jumped at the chance to humiliate the young man in public.

"Perseus, what gift have you brought to celebrate my marriage? So far, I've received several horses, a house by the sea, a new shield, and bolts of silk for my beautiful new bride!" Polydectes goaded him.

Perseus was young and inexperienced. The king easily deceived Perseus, who was honest and unaccustomed to dealing with liars.

"Why, I could sooner bring you the head of Medusa as to give you a new horse or a house by the sea!" the young man replied.

Perseus had fallen into the king's trap, and the king showed him no mercy. "Then bring me the head of Medusa as my wedding present!" he demanded. "Leave immediately, and never return until you bring back the monster's head!"

Polydectes had won. No mortal could kill Medusa, and both the king and Perseus knew it.

Confused, Perseus turned to leave the gathering. His face burned with embarrassment as laughter erupted from behind.

Standing on the beach, he watched the moon's shimmering reflection stretch south from his feet across the sea and on to the horizon. Medusa was somewhere at the end of the moon's road.

How could he find Medusa?

How could he kill her?

Perseus should not have despaired. From Mount Olympus, the gods were watching. As was the way of the gods, everything Perseus needed to fulfill his rash promise would be revealed in time.

Mount Olympus is the tallest mountain in Greece. Mytikas, its tallest peak, is about 9,570 feet (2,918 meters) high. No one really knows when the ancients began to associate this real peak, located southwest of Thessaloniki, with the mythical Mount Olympus.

Medusa and Her Gorgon Sisters

Medusa was one of three Gorgons, but she was the only mortal one. She could die, but Perseus could not look at her if he hoped to live long enough to kill her.

Medusa

She had started life as a beautiful maiden with glorious hair. She was so beautiful that the god of the sea, Poseidon, fell madly in love with her. Instead of accepting or refusing his advances, she teased him unmercifully. Poseidon was crazy with love and chased Medusa all over the city of Athens.

Medusa finally sought refuge in Athena's temple. Poseidon cared nothing for Athena's sanctuary and surged in after the woman. The temple filled with salt water and all manner of sea life.

When Poseidon finally left and the waters receded, Athena found her temple in ruins. The pair had spoiled her holy temple. In her anger, the goddess turned Medusa into a Gorgon.

The Gorgons were hideous female monsters with huge piglike teeth and brass claws. Golden scales covered their bodies. Their claim to fame was their horrific hair. Instead of locks of silk, live snakes grew from their scalp. The snakes slithered and hissed in a writhing, tangled mess.

Poseidon could not bear to look at his transformed lover. He banished her to the Libyan Desert, where she lived with her two Gorgon sisters, Stheno (STHEE-noh) and Euryale (yoo-RY-uh-lee). Medusa was the ugliest of the three.[2] Anyone having the misfortune to look upon her instantly turned to stone. Statues of animals and people unlucky enough to catch a glimpse of her littered the dark, damp cave she called home.

Modern writers believe the Gorgons represented the terrors of the sea. Specifically, the sisters personified the strong winds and currents of the ocean's open waters.[3]

14

Perseus and the Sea Nymphs, painted by Edward Coley Burne-Jones in 1877. Poseidon's daughters the sea nymphs had a special task: to guard the Pack of Pluto. When the time came, they handed over the pack, with magic shoes, helmet, and wallet, to Perseus.

PERSEUS

Perseus,
The Gorgon Slayer

In the dark moments following the king's betrayal, Perseus took heart. A soft breeze blew in from the north and coaxed the trees to sing. The twittering leaves seemed to repeat, "The Graeae, seek the Gray Sisters."

Perseus didn't know where the idea had come from, but if the Gray Sisters could help him find Medusa, he must start there. The only problem was that he didn't know who the Gray Sisters were or where they lived. Finding them might prove just as difficult as finding Medusa.

As the sun rose, he walked to Athena's temple. At her altar, he lay facedown on the floor to pray. After a long while, he opened his eyes to rise and saw a bright object. On the altar steps, he found a metal shield, polished to a brilliant finish. As he stood over the shield, his reflection stared back—the shield was a perfect mirror. Under the shield, he found a curved sword, a scimitar. He would recognize it anywhere—it was the sword of Hermes (HUR-meez), the messenger of the gods!

For the first time, he realized that the gods must be with him in his quest. Perseus thanked them for their gifts.

From Athena's altar, Perseus traveled to the oracle at Delphi, who answered with more of a riddle than an answer: "Search for the people who do not eat Demeter's golden grain, but only acorns." Perseus knew that Demeter (DIH-mih-ter) was the goddess of the harvest, but he didn't know anybody who ate acorns.

His journey took him to the land of Dodona (doh-DOH-nuh), where the Selli (SEH-lee) made their bread from acorns, not wheat. They were happy people and they celebrated everything. The Selli

welcomed Perseus. They had both good and bad news for him. They couldn't help him find the Gray Sisters, who were actually sisters to the Gorgons. However, the Selli were priests to Zeus. They confided to Perseus that he and his journey had found favor with the gods.

Being under the gods' protection was certainly good news, but Perseus was no closer to the Gray Sisters than before. At least that's what he thought. In despair, he began to wander aimlessly, but as the Selli had said, the gods were with him—quite literally. As he walked, Perseus found he was no longer alone. A strange and beautiful man carrying a wand of gold with wings at one end was walking beside him. Perseus knew him immediately by the winged hat and sandals that he wore. Hermes, messenger of the gods, was beside him!

"Perseus, you must prepare to meet Medusa. The Nymphs of the North have everything you need." With that, Hermes took Perseus by the hand, and together they flew into the north.

The pair flew to the edge of the world, where it is always twilight. In the land of gray skies, Perseus found the three old sisters. More surprisingly, the three sisters were huge swans with human heads and gray feathers. As they flitted about, Perseus caught sight of human arms and hands beneath their wings.

They were so old that they had just one eye and one tooth left among them, both of which they shared. Following Hermes' advice, Perseus remained hidden until the sisters passed the eye. Just then, he sprang from his hiding spot and snatched the eye.

After a moment, the sisters began to cackle at one another.

"Sister! Give me the eye, it's my turn!" one wailed.

"Whatever do you mean, I just handed you the eye."

"I didn't take it."

"I didn't either," said the third.

For a moment, the three sisters were quiet. Each thought that the other sister had the eye.

"Sisters! We have lost the eye!" they all shouted.

With that, the three began digging and clawing at the dirt, searching for their lone eye. They honked and yelled as gray feathers flew.

Hermes accompanied Perseus to find the Gray Sisters and the Nymphs of the North.

Perseus stood and watched. He gave them just enough time to become desperate.

"Ladies, are you looking for this?" he finally yelled above their honking and hollering.

The three fell silent.

"What do you have?" they asked. They were, after all, very suspicious of him, and with good reason.

"Why, I have a huge ugly old eyeball. Is it yours?"

"Yes! Yes!" They cackled. "Give it to us!"

Perseus had them just where he wanted them. As Hermes had predicted, they would do anything to get their eye back.

"Tell me where I can find the Nymphs of the North. I need their help to kill the Gorgon Medusa."

The sisters weren't keen on giving up the location of the nymphs.

"I'll toss your eye into the sea for fish food!" Perseus threatened.

"No!" the three sisters wailed.

Defeated, they clumped together and sighed. One sister finally spoke, giving Perseus the directions he sought.

Perseus turned his back on the three. When he was far enough away to feel safe, he threw the eye back at them. He watched the feathers and dust fly. Hermes took his hand, and they left the twilit sky behind. (Ovid wrote that Perseus snatched just the eye. In some later versions, he snatched the eye and the tooth.)

Hermes took Perseus to an isolated sea cave. Inside, Perseus found three nymphs. All three were as young and beautiful as the Gray Sisters had been old and ugly. Knowing nothing of the world of men, the

nymphs didn't know enough to be afraid of Perseus. In fact, they found him a lovely creature and liked him very much.

Perseus spent the next few hours in the cave telling the nymphs stories about men. He described cities, animals, war, and even parties. After they had exhausted his knowledge of the world beyond their cave, Perseus remembered his quest.

"I have promised to kill Medusa. Hermes has brought me here to claim the tools you hold for me."

Hearing those words, the nymphs retrieved a hidden pack and handed it to him. It was the Pack of Pluto, and it had been their job since the beginning of time to protect it. From this pack, Perseus took what he would need to slay Medusa: a pair of winged sandals, a helmet, and a wallet.

Perseus put on the sandals and found himself hovering over the floor of the cave. Like Hermes, he now had a pair of flying shoes. After putting on the helmet, the nymphs could not see him. They began to shout for him until he took it off. Anyone wearing the helmet was invisible. At first, the wallet was a bit of a mystery, but he soon learned that it would hold any object, large or small. He would carry Medusa's severed head back to Seriphos in the wallet.

Perseus was now ready to take on Medusa, but he still didn't know where she lived, and neither did the nymphs. Fortunately, Hermes did. He led Perseus over the sea to the Libyan Desert in North Africa. Perseus was surprised that anything lived in the unrelenting heat and glare of the Libyan sun.

As they approached the Gorgons' lair, Hermes warned Perseus not to look at Medusa. They flew in low and hovered behind one of the many rocks that surrounded the Gorgons' cave.

Perseus shuddered when he saw that the rock he was hiding behind was really the stone remains of a man. The legend, then, was true. All about them were the statues of unlucky creatures whose only crime had been to gaze upon Medusa.

All was quiet, as the three Gorgon sisters were asleep. The gods surely were with Perseus that day.

Perseus used his shield to view the sisters, who were more hideous than he had imagined. Even asleep, they were terrible. Perseus saw a confused mess of bat wings, pig snouts, sharp tusks, swollen tongues, and bulging eyelids that oozed with mucus. The mass of twisted, hissing, scaly green snakes was terrifying. The slithering serpents struck at anything that moved, including one another.

Wearing the helmet, he moved in and hovered unseen over the sisters. Using the shield, he watched them sleep. He had only one problem. Which Gorgon was Medusa? The other two were immortal. A blow to the wrong sister would simply wake them all up. Even invisible, he would have trouble escaping all three of them.

At that moment, Athena joined Perseus. She pointed to the Gorgon lying in the middle of the pile and said, "That one is Medusa." Athena was still on a personal vendetta against Medusa for defiling her temple. She had a reason for wanting to see Medusa dead.

There was nothing left for Perseus to do but strike. Knowing he had only one chance, he gazed into the shield and lifted the sword. Athena, guiding his hand, made sure that his cut was quick and precise. With a single stroke, he sliced through Medusa's neck, severing her head from her shoulders.

His shield revealed a repulsive sight—at Medusa's neck, a pool of blood was forming. A brilliant white lump washed out and lay in the blood. Through his shield, Perseus watched as the lump changed. A beautiful white horse unfolded its legs, stood up, and finally spread a set of huge wings. (Some sources claim Pegasus and Chrysaor were both born at the time—from drops of Medusa's blood that fell into the sea as Perseus flew away. Apollonius wrote that drops of blood created a new species of desert serpent.)

Medusa had been pregnant. The flying horse, Pegasus (PEH-guh-sus), was her child by Poseidon.

Just then, the blood-spattered sisters woke up. Perseus' blood ran cold with their shrieks. He had no time to lose. Quickly, he flew off, stuffing the gory head of Medusa into his magic wallet. He took great care not to look at it. Even dead, Medusa's ugliness was still lethal.

American painter John Singer Sargent shows Perseus astride Pegasus as the hero slays Medusa. Other versions of the myth say Pegasus was born from Medusa's blood—after she was slain.

He had done it! He had killed Medusa. Now he could return home victorious. Still wearing his winged sandals, he headed north for home. As is often the case, though, the gods weren't quite finished with Perseus. Only in their time would he reach his destination.

The Greek Oracles

The ancient Greeks believed in many gods and goddesses. To them, the gods were super humans with total control over mortal men. The Greeks honored their deities in ornate temples. Usually, a temple honored just one god.

Some temples were known for their oracles—women who could foretell the future (or so the ancient Greeks believed). The most famous

Oracle of Delphi temple ruins

oracle was at Delphi. Both King Acrisius and Perseus consulted this oracle.

The faithful waited outside in the heat for hours. They paid huge fees for just a few moments with her. Once inside, one by one, they took a narrow staircase down to a small chamber. A partition separated the faithful from the priestess, known as the Pythia. From her side of the partition, the Pythia responded to questions. She showed no emotion and used a language that only the attending priest or priestess understood.

An ancient legend attributed the trancelike state to fumes that rose from the chamber floor through a crack in the earth.[1] Plutarch, a high priest in the first century CE, wrote that the gas had a sweet odor.[2] Historians doubted his story for centuries.

A recent geological study found two intersecting faults just below the ruins of the Delphic temple. The interaction between these two major faults made it easier for the water and gas below the surface to escape into the temple.[3]

An analysis of the bedrock under the temple found sediments high in hydrocarbon deposits, known as ethylene. This sweet-smelling gas acts as a narcotic when inhaled. The effects produce euphoria and the sense of leaving one's body. These findings don't support the prophetic claims of the oracles, but it could explain the trancelike state and unintelligible language they spoke.

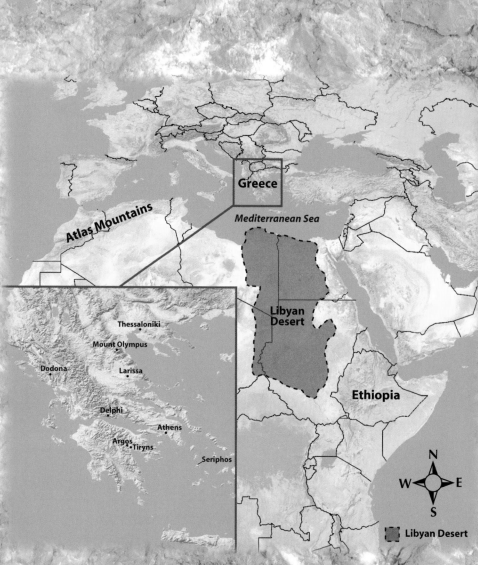

Greece

Atlas Mountains

Mediterranean Sea

Libyan
Desert

Thessaloniki

Mount Olympus

Dodona

Larissa

Delphi

Athens

Argos • Tiryns

Seriphos

Ethiopia

N

W ✦ E

S

Libyan Desert

Perseus traveled several miles during his adventures. The sea took him from Argos, on
the mainland, to the tiny island of Seriphos. In pursuit of Medusa, he traveled through
the Libyan Desert, in north Africa, and then to Ethiopia.

PERSEUS

CHAPTER 4

Andromeda's Hero

Perseus had won. Now fishermen would sing songs about him, the Medusa slayer! It didn't take long for his adventure to catch up with him. Near nightfall, he began to look for a quiet place to sleep through the night.

He spotted a delightful island with herds of grazing sheep and goats. Perseus landed in an enchanted garden. It held a spectacular tree bearing golden apples. Even in the last moments of twilight, the tree sparkled.

Perseus was just drifting off to sleep when the ground quaked and a voice from the sky bellowed, "Who are you and why are you here?"

Through sleepy eyes, Perseus saw a giant holding up the sky with his huge hands. Although the heavens were heavy, it wasn't the giant's heaviest burden. Fear was. Just like King Acrisius, an oracle had warned him that one day a son of Zeus would kill him.

"I only mean to rest for the night. I didn't know anyone lived on the island. I apologize for intruding. May I stay the night?" Perseus asked.

Thus, Atlas, the immense giant, and Perseus, the Medusa slayer, struck up a friendly conversation. Atlas found it hard to believe that a mortal man had slain the infamous Medusa. "How could a mere mortal slay the hideous Medusa?" he asked.

"I am the son of Zeus," Perseus replied. "I'm sure I had the help of the gods today."

That was probably the worst thing Perseus could have said. Atlas reacted poorly.

"Liar! You're a liar!" Atlas spat at the mortal sitting near his feet. "Get off my island before I smash you like the worm you are!"

Atlas wasn't angry because he thought Perseus was lying. In fact, the giant was terribly afraid that the young man was telling the truth. He had to frighten him away before he had a chance to kill him, as the oracle had foretold.

The oracle had warned Atlas that a son of Zeus would kill him. Perseus didn't like it when Atlas tried to frighten him, so he killed the giant by showing him Medusa's hideous head.

Perseus could have just left, but he did not. The giant's taunt offended him. Atlas was too strong for Perseus to fight, but the hero had Medusa's head. He reached into his magic wallet and held the head high. Atlas stared at the snake-topped head, and it was the last thing he ever did. The giant's beard and hair sprouted trees and turned into a huge forest growing high upon the summit that had been the giant's head. His arms formed high cliffs atop the huge mountain that had once been his body. He stands there even still, as the Atlas Mountains, supporting the heavens and all its stars.[1]

While Perseus slept at the foot of the new mountains, a tragic event was unfolding that would change his future. Completely unknown to him, in a land nearby, another hideous monster was plundering the African kingdom of Ethiopia (ee-thee-OH-pee-ah). Daily, Cetus (SEE-tus) rose from the sea and stalked the city. The citizens sacrificed goats and pigs, but the animal flesh didn't appease the monster.

In desperation, the king, Cepheus (SEE-fee-us), consulted the African oracle. What could he do to appease the sea monster? The oracle's reply was more frightening than the monster: "Only your daughter, Andromeda [an-DRAH-muh-dah], will satisfy the sea creature. Adorn her in her finest jewels and chain her to the seaside cliff. Once the monster devours her, he will return to the deep waters of the ocean and bother you no more."

"No! Not Andromeda! Anyone but Andromeda!" King Cepheus cried out in anguish.

The oracle was unmoved by the king's pleas. "Poseidon demands this sacrifice in return for Queen Cassiopeia's [kah-see-oh-PEE-uh] grievous insult of his daughters, the sea nymphs. If you fail to satisfy Poseidon, the monster will destroy you all, one bite at a time."

The king had no choice. He loved his daughter, but he had his entire kingdom to protect.

A sad procession dragged the terrified princess to the cliffs. Andromeda begged for mercy as soldiers chained her to the rock. They turned their backs on her and left. She would have to face the monster alone.

She sobbed silently, for there was no one to hear her. Waves crashed against the cliff. Soon she was wet and cold, besides being terrified. Except for her tears, she made no sound or movement.

From the sky, Perseus spotted the maiden chained

Poseidon, god of the sea, never meets Perseus, but he certainly impacts the story. After Poseidon and Medusa defiled Athena's temple, Athena turned Medusa into a Gorgon. It is Poseidon's daughters, the sea nymphs, who give Perseus the Pack of Pluto. He sent Cetus to Cepheus' kingdom after his wife, Cassiopeia, insulted his beautiful sea nymphs.

to a rock. Hovering close by, he watched in disbelief as the wind blew her hair and the waves drenched her body. Slowly, he drifted around to face her. Andromeda's eyes opened wide in fear. The instant their eyes met, Perseus fell madly in love with her.

Perseus patiently listened while Andromeda told her sad story. Queen Cassiopeia had bragged that she was more beautiful than the sea nymphs, the daughters of Poseidon. Everyone knew she was playing a dangerous game with the gods. Claiming to be superior to any god led straight to doom. The queen had been too stupid and vain to care a wit for the gods or their fury.

To retaliate, Poseidon sent a sea monster to terrorize the kingdom. Every day it left the sea and preyed on the citizens. The bones of the dead littered the streets.

As she neared the end of her woeful tale, they heard the sound of waves breaking and felt the earth rumble. A quick look proved their worst fears. The monster was rising from the ocean. Andromeda screamed in terror and began to struggle against her chains.

"If I slay the monster, will you marry me?" Perseus asked the princess.

She stared in disbelief and then nodded quickly. Of course she would marry him.

With that, Perseus soared into the air and came at the monster from behind. He plunged his sword deep into the monster's neck, just between its shoulders. In pain, the enraged beast reared suddenly and then plunged into the water. The monster writhed from side to side, but Perseus was relentless. The monster's scales were tough, so Perseus lashed at the fleshiest spots. He pierced the monster from the top of his shoulders to the tip of his tail.[2]

Soon the water was dark with the monster's blood. A crowd gathered just in time to watch the monster gasp its dying breath and roll over dead.

The crowd roared and clapped as Perseus unchained the princess and scooped her up in his arms. Together, the pair flew over the crowd

Perseus Frees Andromeda, painted by Piero di Cosimo around 1515. Perseus wasted no time killing Cetus, the sea monster. In return, he won the hand of the beautiful Andromeda in marriage. Through her, his descendants ruled the kingdom of Ethiopia.

and home to the palace. Andromeda's parents were overjoyed and immediately ordered a wedding feast.

One would think that Perseus and Andromeda lived happily ever after, but they did not. Andromeda's betrothed, Phineus (FIH-nee-us), disrupted this festival of love and forgiveness. He was furious to find his intended bride sharing dinner with her new husband.

King Cepheus admonished Phineus, "You should have claimed her when she lay chained to the rock!" As far as the king was concerned, since Phineus had left Andromeda to die, the engagement was off. Phineus didn't like the king's decision and threw a javelin at Perseus. He missed. Just then, a band of men loyal to Phineus attacked the wedding party and their guests.

Perseus and Andromeda, painted by Pierre Mignard in 1679. Everyone rejoiced when Perseus saved Andromeda and killed the horrible Cetus. King Cepheus and Queen Cassiopeia gladly agreed to a marriage between their daughter and Perseus.

"Friends! Turn your eyes away quickly!" shouted Perseus. All complied except Phineus and his men, to their own peril. Perseus held Medusa's head high and Phineus and his men stopped—stone-cold dead.

Soon, the happy couple left for Seriphos, as Perseus had unfinished business there. Once he gave Medusa's head to Polydectes, he could put aside his hero life. He and Andromeda could settle down and raise a family—or so he thought.

The gods still had plans for Perseus. They would be finished when they were finished.

Myths and Constellations

After her death, Queen Cassiopeia took her place among the stars as the constellation Cassiopeia, The Lady in the Chair. The sea nymphs never completely forgave her and placed her near the North Pole. In that position, she spends half the night standing on her head. By placing her there, they hoped to teach her humility.

All the characters in the Perseus myth have constellations of their own. Most can be seen from the Northern Hemisphere during the spring or fall. We'll never know whether Perseus' legend arose from the constellations or whether the legends inspired the naming of the constellations. William Olcott suggests that the constellations honor the legend: ". . . the constellation Perseus, rising before Andromeda, seems to deliver it from the night, which might well be depicted as a monster, such as appears in the figure on the constellation Cetus."[3] It does appear that the constellations were designed with intent and not at random.

Modern astronomers believe that ancient Babylonian astronomers invented Perseus around 1433 BCE.[4] By the fifth century BCE, the story was firmly entrenched in ancient mythology. Euripides and Sophocles, both Greek writers, wrote about Andromeda in the fifth century.

The most notable star in Perseus is Algol, a blinking star. It's actually part of a binary star system, and one star regularly blocks the other. This makes the star appear to blink. In Perseus, Algol represents Medusa's head. Others have called it Demon Star and Blinking Demon.[5]

Perseus, Cassiopeia, and Andromeda in the night sky

The Baleful Head, by Sir Edward Burne-Jones, painted around 1887. Perseus allows Andromeda to gaze into a pool of water to see the reflection of Medusa's severed head. Even in death, Medusa's ugliness is still powerful enough to kill. Perseus used her head to kill Atlas, Phineus, and King Polydectes.

PERSEUS

Perseus Fulfills His Fate

The happy couple found no one at home when they reached Seriphos. Clymene had died during his absence. His mother and Dictys were hiding from Polydectes in Athena's temple.

While Perseus was gone, Danaë continued to refuse the king until finally he turned to force. He sent soldiers to find her, with orders to drag her back to the palace if necessary. The soldiers found only an empty hut by the sea. Dictys and Danaë had sought sanctuary in Athena's temple. Soon, Polydectes discovered them there.

Perseus arrived home not a minute too soon. Even as he and his new wife landed, soldiers were surrounding the temple with drawn swords. Polydectes walked toward the temple. He stopped to pluck a spear from the sand.

If Danaë didn't come out on her own, Polydectes would hunt them down and kill Dictys. He'd kill Danaë, too, if it came to that. She had humiliated him long enough. He entered the temple and shouted, "Danaë! You can't hide forever. Come out now or I'll kill Dictys."

Deep inside the sanctuary, Dictys and Danaë heard Polydectes. There was no place else for them to hide. Danaë knew what she must do: "Dictys, I must go out to him. I won't let him kill you. I'd rather marry him than lose you."

Dictys tried to argue with her, but even he knew it was hopeless. He couldn't fight the soldiers or even Polydectes alone. He was an old man now.

Their sorrowful goodbye was interrupted by an unseen voice: "Close your eyes, and don't open them again until I tell you." They didn't know who was whispering to them, but they were in the temple, so they obeyed without question.

Perseus took off his helmet in clear view of Polydectes. When the king saw that the young man carried no shield or sword, he laughed. "So, you have returned at last. I banished you until you returned with Medusa's head! Prepare to die!" He raised his spear, but he never got a chance to launch it. Perseus turned his head and pulled Medusa's head from his magic wallet.

Polydectes, the king with a heart of stone, suddenly had a body to match.

Perseus returned to his mother and Dictys, who were overjoyed to see him. Despite the danger they had all been in, Perseus was saddened by the sight of the stone king. Too many men had died in his quest to kill Medusa. He was weary of his task.

Perseus walked to the altar and thanked the gods for their help. Then he laid down his shield and sword. Next he took off the winged shoes. Finally he placed the wallet with Medusa's head on the altar. He knew that the gods would reclaim them.

Outside, the people of Seriphos cheered and then knelt before Perseus. He had rid them of the cruel Polydectes. Dictys named Perseus king of Seriphos.

"King Perseus!" the crowd yelled over and over.

Athena watched the crowd from inside. She attached Medusa's head to her breastplate, where it would remain forever. The goddess smiled briefly and then was gone. It is said that she rode a flying white horse from the temple.

Perseus declined to rule the island and made Dictys king in his place. Eventually he would replace Dictys, but he knew he was too young and inexperienced to rule. Besides, there was still a piece of his life missing. He wanted to meet his grandfather, King Acrisius. Perhaps time had softened the old king's heart.

Perseus, Andromeda, and Danaë set sail for Argos. When news reached Argos that Perseus was on his way, Acrisius fled the city in terror. He traveled to Larissa (lah-RIH-sah), where that city's king was hosting the Greek games. Acrisius hid among the athletes and tourists.

Perseus would never find him in the crowded city—or at least, that's what Acrisius thought.

Perseus was disappointed to find the king gone. It was his fate, he told himself. If his grandfather hadn't cast him out to sea, he'd have never grown up in Seriphos. He'd have never gone on his quest to kill Medusa, nor would he have met Andromeda. He tried to be content.

From Argos, the trio traveled to Larissa to enjoy the games. They were not purposely following Acrisius, as they had no idea where the old king had gone. They had simply decided to make the best of their journey.

By this time, everyone knew of Perseus, even the citizens of Larissa. As the famous Medusa slayer, Perseus enjoyed every luxury and kindness the people had to offer. During the festivities, he and Andromeda watched the tanned young men compete. From their balcony in the palace, they could see the tourists and hear the music that filled the streets.

One afternoon, Perseus and Andromeda joined the prince of Larissa as his guest at one of the games. On impulse, the prince invited Perseus to compete in the discus competition. Perseus accepted.

As he walked into the dusty arena, he heard the prince announce him: "I give you Perseus, the Medusa slayer!"

Perseus took a moment to scan the cheering crowd. He shielded his eyes from the sun and sought the face of his lovely wife. There she was, standing next to the prince. It was remarkable how far he had come. Here he stood, before a cheering crowd of his fellow Greeks. He was no longer a castoff, he and his children were the heirs to Ethiopia, Seriphos, and perhaps even Argos someday.

Perseus tightened his grip on the discus and started to spin. Despite his humble childhood, he was an excellent athlete. At the end of the spin, he let the discus fly. It was a tremendous throw and the crowd cheered—and then abruptly fell silent. He had thrown too hard. The discus had overshot the field and flown into the crowd of startled spectators.

Perseus heard the quick gasps of alarmed fans. The discus had struck an old man in the head. Perseus ran into the stands, but he was too late. There was nothing he could do. The old man lay dead.

"King Acrisius!" he heard from nearby. "He's killed the king of Argos!"

Perseus couldn't move. Horrified, he looked at the old man lying dead at his feet. He had killed his own grandfather.

When the shock passed, Perseus cried out in grief. For three days, he shut himself up alone in the palace. No one could console him.

No one blamed Perseus for the king's death.[1] It was his fate, everyone said. Everyone knew that the king had cast Perseus into the sea in an effort to escape his fate. Hadn't the oracle predicted the event years ago? Mortal men could not change their fate. Everyone but Perseus thought of the king's death as a sign.

(This ending is the most popular, but not part of Ovid's original poem. In Ovid's version, Perseus restores his dethroned grandfather to his kingdom. Later, he accidentally hits Acrisius in the head and kills him.)

Perseus and his family took the king's body back to Argos. As Perseus entered the city, the citizens cheered and threw flowers at him. They were glad the reign of Acrisius was over. He had been a cruel and thoughtless king.

The ministers of Argos tried to persuade Perseus to rule over the kingdom. In his grief, he refused. Finally, his cousin Megapenthes (meh-guh-PEN-theez) in Tiryns (tih-RINZ) made him an offer he couldn't refuse. The two heirs switched kingdoms. Megapenthes would rule Argos, and Perseus would rule Tiryns.

Once he had fulfilled his fate, the gods were finally finished with him, and not one minute too soon for Perseus. Left to live as he chose, he enjoyed a long and happy life with Andromeda. Eventually, the small kingdom of Tiryns grew into the great civilization of Mycenae (my-SEE-nee).

Together, Perseus and Andromeda had five sons: Electryon (ee-LEK-tree-on), Alcaeus (AL-see-us), Perses (PER-seez), Sthenelus (STHEH-

The ancient ruins of Argos lie along the edge of modern Argos. According to the myth, Perseus was born in the Greek city of Argos to the daughter of King Acrisius. Depending on the version you read, he spent only a few months to years in Argos. He returned after his marriage to find his grandfather. Modern Argos is a popular tourist attraction.

nuh-lus), and Mestor (MES-tor). These children lived on to rule kingdoms in North Africa and Greece. The Persians took their name from Perses, and their kings claimed to be his descendants. Sthenelus became a king of Mycenae. Little is known about Mestor.

Electryon married Anaxo (ah-NAK-soh), Alcaeus' daughter. Alcaeus also had a son, Amphitryon (am-FIH-tree-on), who later killed Electryon by accident. While recovering stolen cattle, Amphitryon threw a club at a cow and hit Electryon instead. For his crime, he was exiled from Mycenae.[2]

House of Perseus

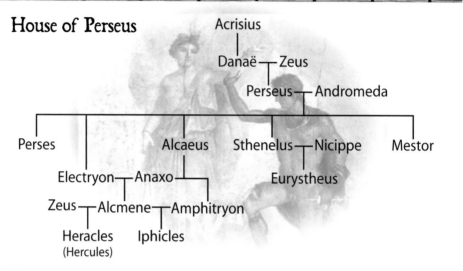

No version of the Perseus myth identifies Danaë's mother. It seems that she was King Acrisius' only child. Perseus and Andromeda had five sons. According to some, they also had a daughter, Gorgophone (gor-GAH-fuh-nee), whose name means "killing of the Gorgon." One of their descendants, Hercules, is the most famous of all the Greek heroes.

Electryon and Anaxo had a daughter, Alcmene (alk-MEE-nee). She, with Zeus, produced the most famous hero of the Greek myths, Heracles (known now by his Roman name, Hercules). Alcmene has the distinction of being the last mortal woman Zeus bothered.[3] Hercules' twin brother, Iphicles (IH-fih-kleez), was mortal: He was the offspring of Amphitryon, Alcmene's husband.

Hera was jealous as usual and sent two large snakes to kill Hercules. Less than a year old, he squeezed the serpents to death. Thus begins the story of the most famous Greek hero of all. It began just as the fate willed it.

The story of Perseus isn't restricted to Greek mythology. His supernatural birth, a grandfather's fear of being supplanted, the Medusa-witch, divine gifts of weapons, and even the sacrifice of a princess like Andromeda occur in ancient stories around the globe. Greek storytelling reveals an ancient world we might not otherwise know. Today, we try to explain the similarities among ancient myths. There are many. Perhaps all cultures rose from a single source. Or perhaps human psychology managed to create the stories from life issues, such as birth, survival, and death. Regardless of how they came to be, the Greek myths are some of the best.

Of all the ancient heroes of myth and legend, Perseus stands out. His intentions are good and he is successful in all quests. He never falls from glory and keeps the gods on his side from beginning to end. When his adventure is over, he puts aside his weapons and lives in peace. He is the archetype for subsequent heroes.

From his adventures, we know a great deal about the ancient Greek world. Kings were all powerful, women had few if any rights, the people valued material possessions, and they rejected human sacrifice. Perhaps most important, they were a courageous people who faced their fate—good or bad.

The story of Perseus isn't just for the ancient Greeks. His story is one of collaboration, innovation, and mature, responsible reactions to trying times. The Perseus myth is as relevant today as it was thousands of years ago.

The Timing

No version of the Perseus myth offers direct references to when the story is said to have occurred. Because the mythological Perseus supposedly founded the city of Mycenae, scholars believe that the Perseus myth originated in Mycenaean times. Perseus is certainly the most famous hero of Mycenae. The story takes great care to credit him with the city's founding. Whether an existing story was adapted to connect Perseus to the city, we don't know.

However, there are several clues that scholars have used to deduce an approximate period. The first is the use of the metal bronze. King Acrisius uses bronze bars to trap Danaë in her underground chamber. That places the story in one of the three bronze ages:

- Early Bronze Age (3500–2000 BCE)
- Middle Bronze Age (2000–1600 BCE)
- Late Bronze Age (1600–1200 BCE)[4]

Other versions of the story claim the chest in which Perseus and Danaë drifted to Seriphos was bronze. In addition, many versions describe the shield Athena gave to Perseus as polished bronze.

Another clue is the powerful and often competing kingdoms mentioned throughout the story: Argos, Seriphos, Delphi, and Tiryns. These city kingdoms are characteristic of the Middle and Late Bronze Ages in ancient Greece.

Perhaps the most important clue is the reference to Mycenae. According to the legend, Perseus trades his rightful kingdom of Argos with his cousin. Then he founds the Greek kingdom of Mycenae. Historically, civilization first felt the influence of the Mycenaean empire around 1600 BCE. The emergence of Mycenae puts Perseus right at the beginning of the Late Bronze Age, around 1600 BCE.[5]

Mycenae reconstruction

CHAPTER NOTES

Chapter 1. A Supernatural Birth

1. Homer, *Iliad,* translated by Robert Fagles (New York: Penguin Books, 1991), 16: 459–461.

Chapter 2. Out of the Sea

1. Edith Hamilton, *Mythology* (Boston: Little, Brown, and Company, 1942), p. 143.

2. Donald Richardson, *Hercules and Other Legends of Gods and Heroes* (New York: Gramercy Books, 1996), p. 77.

3. Thomas Bulfinch, *Bulfinch's Mythology* (New York: Random House, 1998), pp. 120–121.

Chapter 3. Perseus, the Gorgon Slayer

1. John Roach, "Delphic Oracle's Lips May Have Been Loosened by Gas Vapors," *National Geographic News,* August 14, 2001, http://news. nationalgeographic.com/ news/2001/08/0814_delphioracle. html

2. Ibid.

3. Ibid.

Chapter 4. Andromeda's Hero

1. Donald Richardson, *Hercules and Other Legends of Gods and Heroes* (New York: Gramercy Books, 1996), p. 11.

2. Ibid., pp. 78–79.

3. William Tyler Olcott, *Star Lore of All Ages* (New York and London: G. P. Putnam's Sons, 1911), p. 302.

4. Ibid.

5. Ibid., p. 303

Chapter 5. Perseus Fulfills His Fate

1. Jay MacPherson, *Four Ages of Man: The Classical Myths* (New York: St. Martin's Press, 1962), p. 59.

2. Donald Richardson, *Hercules and Other Legends of Gods and Heroes* (New York: Gramercy Books, 1996), p. 175.

3. J. E. Zimmerman, *Dictionary of Classical Mythology* (New York: Harper & Row Publishers, 1964), p. 16.

4. Ibid., pp. 170–171.

5. Ibid., p. 171.

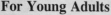

For Young Adults

Burns, Lucilla. *Greek Myths*. Avon, England: The Bath Press, 1990.

Evans, Cheryl, and Anne Millard. *Greek Myths and Legends*. London: Usborne Publishing Ltd., 1985.

Gibson, Michael. *Gods, Men & Monsters*. New York: Schocken Books, 1982.

Low, Alice. *Greek Gods and Heroes*. New York: Macmillan Publishing Company, 1985.

McCaughrean, Geraldine. *Perseus*. Chicago: Cricket Books, 2003.

Ross, Stewart. *Daily Life*. Chicago: Peter Bedrick Books, Inc., 1999.

Sullivan, K. E. *Greek Myths & Legends*. London: Brockhampton Press, 1998.

Williams, Marcia. *Greek Myths for Young Children*. Cambridge, Massachusetts: Candlewick Press, 1991.

Works Consulted

Bulfinch, Thomas. *Bulfinch's Mythology*. New York: Random House, 1998.

Fiske, John. *Myths and Myth-Makers: Old Tales and Superstitions Interpreted by Comparative Mythology*. Boston and New York: Houghton Mifflin Company, 1914.

Hamilton, Edith. *Mythology*. Boston: Little, Brown and Company, 1942.

Hartland, Edwin Sidney. *The Legend of Perseus: A Study of Tradition in Story Custom and Belief*. London: David Nutt. Strand, 1894.

Homer. *The Iliad*. Translated by Robert Fagles. New York: Penguin Books, 1991.

MacPherson, Jay. *Four Ages of Man: The Classical Myths*. New York: St. Martin's Press, 1962.

Morford, Mark P.O., and Robert J. Lenardon. *Classical Mythology*. New York: Longman, Inc., 1977.

Olcott, William Tyler. *Star Lore of All Ages*. New York and London: G. P. Putnam's Sons, 1911.

Pomeroy, Sarah, Walter Donlan, Stanley M. Burstein, Jennifer Tolbert Roberts. *Ancient Greece: A Political, Social, and Cultural History*. New York: Oxford University Press, 1999.

Richardson, Donald. *Hercules and Other Legends of Gods and Heroes*. New York: Gramercy Books, 1996.

Roach, John. "Delphic Oracle's Lips May Have Been Loosened by Gas Vapors." *National Geographic News,* August 14, 2001. http://news.nationalgeographic.com/news/2001/08/0814_delphioracle.html

Zimmerman, J. E. *Dictionary of Classical Mythology*. New York: Harper & Row Publishers, 1964.

On the Internet

Delphi: In Brief http://iam.classics. unc.edu/loci/16/16_images.html

Perseus http://www.classicsunveiled. com/mythnet/html/perseus.html

Mycenae, Greek Mythology Link http://homepage.mac.com/ cparada/GML/Mycenae.html

MythWeb: Heroes http://www.mythweb.com/ heroes/heroes.html

Constellation Perseus http://www.seds.org/Maps/Stars_ en/Fig/perseus.html

GreekMythology.com http://www. greekmythology.com/

Myth Man's Homework Help Center http://www.thanasis.com/ perseus.htm

Timeless Myths, "Perseus" http://www.timelessmyths.com/ classical/perseus.html

Ancient Greece http://www. ancientgreece.com/

GLOSSARY

archetype (AR-kih-typ)—The original pattern or model of something that is copied.

betrothed (bee-TROH-th'd)—Engaged to be married.

bronze (brawnz)—A metal made of copper and tin.

discus (DIS-kus)—A disk thrown in athletic competitions.

enamor (eh-NAH-mor)—To inspire with love.

fate (FAYT)—A force that controls human lives.

goad (GOHD)—To prod or encourage through trickery or menace.

guise (GIZE)—False appearance or purpose.

lair (LAYER)—An animal's home, usually a cave or hole.

mesmerize (MEZ-mer-yz)—To hypnotize or hold spellbound.

mortal (MOR-tul)—Not a god; one whose life can end.

narcotic (nar-KAH-tik)—A drug or substance that dulls the senses.

oracle (OR-uh-kul)—A person who can tell the future.

personify (pur-SAH-nih-fye)—To represent an abstract idea as a person.

retaliate (ree-TAL-ee-ayt)—To respond in a like manner, usually for revenge.

supplant (suh-PLANT)—To replace, usually through force or strategy.

vendetta (ven-DEH-tuh)—A course of action done for revenge.

wane (WAYN)—To decrease gradually.